The Great BIG Green

Peggy Gifford   Illustrated by Lisa Desimini

BOYDS MILLS PRESS

AN IMPRINT OF HIGHLIGHTS

Honesdale, Pennsylvania

The thing is,

the thing is green.

And the green is,

the green is green.

anaconda green

electric-eel green

green-iguanas-in-the-sun green.

I mean this **thing**
has got **all things green.**
It's got **green turtles**
in **turtle-green** ponds

and a **green tree frog**
on a girl's arm.

It's got green **grasshoppers** springing
from groomed green **lawns**
and green **stinkbugs**
and green **dragonflies**—
it's even got an **old green door**.

And it's got **more**:

it has **dark** and **dangerous** greens

greens-you've-**never-seen** greens

ocean-floor greens

tornado-sky greens

tiger's-eye greens.

It's **chock-full** of green things
that are **good for you:**
your **eat-your-broccoli** greens
your **bunch-of-green-grapes** green

your **watermelons**-sparkling-in-the-sun greens.

This thing leaves **green geckos** on green leaves feeling green

and **green moths** **feeling** in the **green dark**

and green **praying** **mantises** on their **green knees.**

It's a **great** and **gorgeous** green.

A light
bright
just right
watch-it-grow
it-says-**GO**
shade of green.

Have you **guessed** yet?
Do you need **another clue?**

Think rolling-waves-of-grain green

thick green **vines**
climbing high
green trees

mountains and **mountains** of green

billions of **waves** reaching out of dark green **seas**

all
wrapped in one green ball
and hung
like an ornament
in the sky.
What a thing it must be
to see the whole green thing
floating by.

It's true.
The thing is,
the thing is green . . .

. . . except where it's **blue.**

For Susie and J. Patrick Lewis
—PG

For my nephew Jack
—LD

Artist's Note:

For The Great Big Green, I scanned my own paintings, papers, fabric, photos, and some other unusual materials. And then I used these scans to create mixed media collages. For instance, I scanned orange sandpaper, black velvet, and white fur for the tiger. A tiger's-eye stone was used for her eyes. Green marble from Ireland (The Green Island) became tree frogs and small fish. Pipe cleaners became seaweed. I used scans of my own skin for the children's skin and for the large butterfly fish, and I rendered his quickly moving fin from a blurry photo of my hand waving. These are just a few examples. This process is fun for me because I'm always thinking: what else does this object, animal, or person look like, and what can I use to create it?

Boyds Mills Press, An Imprint of Highlights
815 Church Street, Honesdale, Pennsylvania 18431

ISBN: 978-1-62091-629-2. Library of Congress Control Number: 2013947714. First edition. Designed by Barbara Grzeslo. Production by Margaret Mosomillo. The text of this book is set in Frutiger and Typography of Coop. Printed in Malaysia. 10 9 8 7 6 5 4 3 2 1

FSC
www.fsc.org

MIX
Paper from responsible sources
FSC® C012700